ESSENTIAL LIBRARY OF
THE US MILITARY
★ THE US ★
AIR FORCE

Essential Library

An Imprint of Abdo Publishing | www.abdopublishing.com

ESSENTIAL LIBRARY OF
THE US MILITARY
★ THE US ★
AIR FORCE

BY ROBERT GRAYSON

CONTENT CONSULTANT
ROBERT WETTEMANN
DIRECTOR, US AIR FORCE ACADEMY
CENTER FOR ORAL HISTORY

www.abdopublishing.com

Published by Abdo Publishing, a division of ABDO, PO Box 398166, Minneapolis, Minnesota 55439. Copyright © 2015 by Abdo Consulting Group, Inc. International copyrights reserved in all countries. No part of this book may be reproduced in any form without written permission from the publisher. Essential Library™ is a trademark and logo of Abdo Publishing.

Printed in the United States of America, North Mankato, Minnesota
042014
092014

Cover Photo: US Army
Interior Photos: US Army, 2, 52–53, 54, 56, 59, 67, 69, 76–77, 79, 81, 84, 94, 96; Marty Lederhandler/AP Images, 6–7; Adam Butler/AP Images, 14; Daniel M. Silva/ Shutterstock Images, 16–17; North Wind Picture Archives, 23, 24, 27; Bettmann/ Corbis, 28–29; AP Images, 33; US National Archives and Records Administration, 36; Mikami/AP Images, 41; Dominique Mollard/AP Images, 43; Photographer's Mate 1st Class Arlo K. Abrahamson/AP Images, 44–45; US Army/AP Images, 47; US Air Force, 50, 61, 64; Carolina K. Smith/Shutterstock Images, 62–63; Saundra Sovick/The Jonesboro Sun/AP Images, 72; Shutterstock Images, 75; Skryl Sergey/ Shutterstock Images, 86 (top); Christos Georghiou/Shutterstock Images, 86 (bottom); US Department of Defense, 88–89, 100; Red Line Editorial, 93

Editor: Arnold Ringstad
Series Designer: Jake Nordby

Library of Congress Control Number: 2014932857

Cataloging-in-Publication Data

Grayson, Robert.
The US Air Force / Robert Grayson.
p. cm. -- (Essential library of the US military)
ISBN 978-1-62403-432-9
1. United States. Air Force--Juvenile literature.   I. Title.
358.00973--dc23

2014932857

CONTENTS

CHAPTER ONE
AERIAL RESCUE UNDER FIRE

In the early morning hours of October 3, 2009, most of the approximately 60 US Army soldiers at Combat Outpost (COP) Keating were asleep. Suddenly the base, deep in the Afghan mountains near the Pakistan border, was rocked by thunderous blasts.

"That's incoming!" one US soldier yelled, and troops started running for their weapons.[1] Hundreds of fighters belonging to the Taliban, an Afghan insurgent group, were descending on the outpost. The US troops and their Afghan National Army partners were severely outnumbered. Aerial support from the US Air Force offered some hope, but the nearest airbase was more than 100 miles (160 km) away.

Recently Taliban fighters had been attacking COP Keating three or four times a week, but it was usually with a few rounds of small-arms fire and an occasional mortar. But on this day, they seemed determined to overrun the combat outpost and kill everyone inside.

COP Keating was located near Kamdesh, a town in Nuristan Province in eastern Afghanistan. US commanders believed many of the weapons and

THE WAR IN AFGHANISTAN

President George W. Bush declared a war on terror following the September 11, 2001, terrorist attacks against the United States. On that day, terrorists hijacked four planes, crashing three of them into buildings. Passengers on the fourth plane fought back against the hijackers, and the plane crashed in an empty field in the midst of the struggle. In all, the hijackers killed nearly 3,000 people that day.[2] One goal of the war on terror was to track down those responsible for the September 11 attacks. Evidence suggested the leader of terrorist group al-Qaeda, Osama bin Laden, had planned the attack. Bin Laden had been linked to the Taliban, an Islamic fundamentalist group that controlled the Afghan government.

Following the attacks, the United States gave the Taliban an ultimatum to hand over bin Laden and all al-Qaeda leaders. The Taliban refused, and the United States deployed troops to Afghanistan in October to capture terrorists and destroy terrorist training camps. The Taliban government was quickly toppled, but many of its supporters found sanctuary in Pakistan. From there insurgents crossed the border and attacked US soldiers. For more than a decade, insurgents continued to attack US troops. The US military found and killed bin Laden in 2011, but troops remained in Afghanistan.

In the years before the attack, COP Keating hosted local citizens for discussions with the US troops there.

reinforcements for Taliban fighters came through Kamdesh from nearby Pakistan. The job of the troops stationed at COP Keating was to cut off Taliban supply routes while also befriending the native Afghan people who lived in the extremely mountainous region.

Ever since COP Keating was established in 2006, the Taliban had been keeping close watch on it from the mountains that surrounded the 23-building camp on three sides. Now the insurgents were trying to use those mountains to trap and destroy the US and Afghan troops in the area.

The Taliban attacked with rocket-propelled grenades, sniper fire, machine guns, and Russian-made antitank weapons. Many of the Afghan troops abandoned their posts. The US troops fought back with everything they had, but the sheer numbers of the enemy and their positions high above the outpost gave the Taliban a decided advantage. COP Keating was at the bottom of a steep valley, making it difficult to defend against such heavy fire.

At the start of the battle, one of the enemy's grenades hit the camp's generator, leaving the defenders in the dark and forcing them to use batteries to keep their communications equipment going. Hope for assistance from outside the valley was shrinking as the batteries drained. Several US soldiers had already been killed, several others were wounded, and many of the outpost's buildings were on fire.

A PLEA FOR HELP

The soldiers' radio pleas for air support were picked up at Bagram Air Base more than 100 miles (160 km) west of COP Keating. US Air Force Captain Michael Polidor and his weapons system officer, First Lieutenant Aaron Dove, were on the Bagram runway in their two-seat F-15E

Strike Eagle tactical fighter. They had just been cleared for takeoff for a routine mission when they were ordered to change course and head to the battle scene at Keating. It took them approximately 20 minutes to get there.

Meanwhile, the troops at Keating were feverishly holding off the enemy. Insurgents approached from all sides as smoke billowed from the outpost. The defenders repelled one wave of attack after another. Only a barbed-wire fence separated the coalition forces from the Taliban fighters, who were now closing in on the outpost.

Polidor and Dove mentally prepared for the battle ahead as their F-15E streaked toward COP Keating. When they arrived, First Lieutenant Dove peered down on the camp. He later described the chaotic scene below: "You could see the buildings burning. I saw five to eight really

THE F-15E STRIKE EAGLE

The F-15E Strike Eagle is considered one of the most sophisticated fighter planes in the world. It is an improved version of the older F-15 Eagle originally introduced in 1976. The E model adds an extra seat in the cockpit for a person to handle weapon tracking and firing. With the additional seat came new equipment and weapons, giving the plane the ability to handle air-to-ground attacks in addition to its existing air-to-air role. The F-15E carries a wide array of weapons, including bombs, air-to-air missiles, air-to-surface missiles, and an M-61 Vulcan cannon. The fighter's electronic equipment includes systems that can jam an enemy's radar, as well as a warning receiver to detect incoming threats.

The F-15E is among the fastest jets in the air force's arsenal.

large fires going on inside the outpost. And you could see small explosions from the mortars exploding within the outpost and the surrounding hillsides."[3] Two other

F-15Es, also sent to provide air support, had arrived soon before them.

COORDINATING THE ATTACK

As the fighters started dropping bombs and firing at the enemy, Polidor realized the air attack needed to be coordinated. He took control of the situation and started directing the attack from the air. Assessing the battle on the ground, Polidor located multiple enemy positions and orchestrated attacks on the Taliban fighters by the different US aircraft. More aircraft arrived on the scene to offer support.

Polidor also set up a communications relay, guiding US planes through heavy smoke to their targets. The planes soon faced rapidly darkening skies from a fast-moving thunderstorm on the horizon. With Dove's help, Polidor dropped all four of his plane's bombs on the enemy. He also calculated the coordinates for the other planes to drop their bombs, delivering crushing blows to the Taliban fighters.

With the enemy so close to coalition troops, there was little room for error as US planes pounded enemy strongholds. At the peak of the battle, many aircraft— including six F-15s, several A-10 Thunderbolt II attack planes, two AH-64 Apache helicopters, and a B-1 Lancer heavy bomber—were involved in the fight.[4] Polidor and Dove coordinated all of them.

FINISHING THE FIGHT

Refusing to the leave the volatile battle, Captain Polidor arranged for his and other aircraft to be refueled in midair to keep constant pressure on the enemy. He swooped down between the mountains and blasted the enemy with rapid-fire rounds from his plane's M-61 Vulcan cannon, tearing through the Taliban forces. In all, US aircraft fired 170 rounds, inflicting heavy loses on the insurgents.[5]

Even when Polidor and Dove ran out of ammunition, they stayed on the scene and continued to direct the air attack. At one point, Polidor positioned his plane to do a damage assessment on another F-15E that suffered a mechanical problem during the battle. He guided that plane out of the combat zone so it could get safely back to base. By nightfall the battle was over. Eight Americans had been killed, and more than 150 Taliban fighters lay dead in the mountains surrounding COP Keating. The battle proved to be one of the heaviest days of fighting in the War in Afghanistan (2001–present).

More than 30 bombs were dropped on the insurgents by American flyers.[6] Army Sergeant Eric Harder was in the thick of the ground battle at COP Keating. "If it wasn't for our air cover, I don't think we would've made it out of there," he said afterward.[7]

For their efforts during the fighting at COP Keating, Polidor and Dove were both awarded the Distinguished Flying Cross, an award for members of the US armed forces who show extraordinary achievement and heroism during flight. "When I look back on it, I can't believe we orchestrated all that," Captain Polidor said. "But when we were there, it's like people say, all that training just kind of kicks in."[8]

THE AFTERMATH

The day after the battle at COP Keating, US troops combed the surrounding mountains for any Taliban fighters still hiding in the rocky terrain. A few more enemy troops were killed. On October 6, 2009, COP Keating was evacuated. US military officials decided to focus their efforts on more populated areas. All remaining US soldiers were flown out by helicopter, and the camp was permanently closed. The hasty departure did not leave enough time for all the munitions at the outpost to be destroyed or removed. Immediately after the last of the troops evacuated, the US Air Force sent in a B-1 bomber to destroy the camp to prevent Taliban insurgents from looting it.

CHAPTER TWO
AIRBORNE

On July 21, 1861, high above Prince William County, Virginia, inventor Thaddeus S. C. Lowe floated through the sky in a 15,000-cubic-foot (425 cu m) hydrogen-filled balloon.[1] Using flags, he signaled Union troops on the ground, directing them where to fire artillery rounds at the advancing Confederate soldiers

during the First Battle of Bull Run in the American Civil
War (1861–1865). The war, which pitted the Northern
states of the Union against the Southern states of the
Confederacy, featured the first major use of aerial
technology by the US military.

EYE IN THE SKY

While some in Union army balloons relied on flags to signal troops below, during the Civil War others used telegraphs to communicate with ground troops. Telegraphs were the communication tool of the future in the 1860s. The nation's chief balloon pilot, Thaddeus Lowe, developed a way to bring telegraphs aboard the military balloons. Telegraph cables ran from the balloons to the ground. Pilots used the telegraphs to send reports of enemy troop movements as they happened. Sometimes the balloons soared as high as 1,000 feet (300 m) in the sky. The telegraphs ensured the most accurate intelligence from the front lines of the battlefield reached Union generals quickly.

President Abraham Lincoln established the Union Army Balloon Corps in 1861 and put Lowe in charge of it. The corps started out with one balloon, but quickly added another six, along with the pilots to fly them. The Union army used the balloons between 1861 and 1863. Though useful, the balloons proved to be cumbersome and took time to prepare for battle. They were also at the mercy of winds that could carry them miles away from the battlefield. As a result, the Union army lost interest in flight technology. The Union Army Balloon Corps was disbanded in July 1863.

THE WRIGHT BROTHERS

Flight took a giant leap forward on December 17, 1903, when Wilbur and Orville Wright invented the first successful airplane. The US military, however, was not impressed with the Wright brothers' motorized flying machine. In early tests, the Wright brothers' airplane stayed airborne for just a short time. Citing those results, the US War Department felt investing in the invention was a waste of money. In January 1905, the War Department declined an offer to buy airplanes from the Wright brothers. The Wright brothers did not give up, and they continued to perfect their aircraft.

By 1907, the pioneering inventors had built a stronger airplane with a more powerful engine. This newer version

Early demonstrations of the Wright aircraft failed to convince the US government of the importance of military aviation.

captured the attention of British and French government officials, who wanted to see the aircraft in action. The Wright brothers took their airplane to Europe in May 1907. Test runs there generated so much excitement, military leaders in the US War Department were forced to take another look at the flying machine they had once dismissed as impractical.

By February 10, 1908, the Wright brothers reached an agreement to sell one Wright Military Flyer to the US government for $25,000. The next year, the Aeronautical Division of the US Army Signal Corps took delivery of the aircraft. The two-seat biplane was sent to Fort Myer, Virginia, and renamed *Signal Corps Airplane No. 1.* A new chapter in national defense was about to unfold. Benjamin Foulois of the US Army trained himself to fly the airplane, receiving guidance from the Wright brothers by mail. While developing ways to make the plane useful to the military, Foulois pioneered the use of radio and aerial photography.

Meanwhile, shortly after selling the military flyer to the US Army, the Wright brothers signed a contract to sell airplanes to the French government. This sparked an entire airplane-building industry in Europe. Aircraft manufacturers sprang up throughout the continent. These companies capitalized on the designs and flight concepts

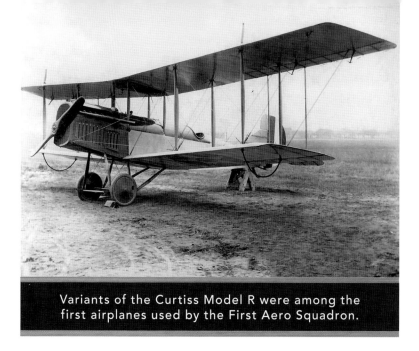

Variants of the Curtiss Model R were among the first airplanes used by the First Aero Squadron.

developed by the Wright brothers and added their own innovative twists.

TURNING PLANES INTO WEAPONS OF WAR

While the US Army planned to use aircraft solely for reconnaissance, France, the United Kingdom, and Germany experimented with ways to mount bombs and guns on the planes and turn them into weapons of war.

Starting in 1910, European nations began making major strides in military aviation. They developed fleets of airplanes and trained pilots to fly them. The US Army was slower to act. Finally, on March 5, 1913, it formed the First Aero Squadron. The unit included nine planes, nine officers who were also pilots, and 51 enlisted men. Even after the US military took this step, the role of an air force in the nation's armed services was still the subject of debate.

As World War I (1914–1918) approached, aviation was underfunded and considered purely experimental by most US military leaders. Many members of the US Congress felt the same way. The nation did not seem interested in developing a strong force to fight a war in the air.

World War I started in Europe on July 28, 1914, and pitted the Allied powers of the United Kingdom, France, Russia, and Italy against the Central powers—Germany, Austria-Hungary, and the Ottoman Empire. In the beginning, the United States stayed out of the war.

Early in the conflict, British aerial reconnaissance helped foil a major enemy

FIRST MISSION

As World War I raged in Europe, a separate conflict closer to home gave the nation's first airborne fighting force a chance to see action. On March 9, 1916, Mexican revolutionary general Pancho Villa, who was having a dispute with the US government, raided the small town of Columbus, New Mexico. His band of guerrilla fighters killed approximately 17 Americans and burned down part of the town.[2]

The US Army was sent into Mexico to track down Villa and his men. The First Aero Squadron provided support for the operation. The squadron conducted reconnaissance missions and flew supplies from the United States to US troops stationed in Mexico.

offensive. But airplanes soon took on additional tasks beyond reconnaissance. Just a few months after the war started, battles between rival nations' aircraft became commonplace in the skies over Europe. Engineers attached machine guns to the front of airplanes. The guns were synchronized to the planes' propellers, allowing pilots to fire straight ahead without damaging their planes. Aerial duels between pilots became as known as dogfights.

US FLYERS IN WORLD WAR I

Even while most Americans were reluctant for the nation to enter World War I, there were some adventurous young men who were ready to answer the call on their own. In April 1916, the French government agreed to start the

FORGOTTEN HERO

More than 200 Americans volunteered to fly for the French Air Service during World War I. One of them was Eugene Bullard of Columbus, Georgia. Born in 1894 during a time of severe racial discrimination in the United States, Bullard went to France in 1913 as an African-American teenager seeking equality. When World War I broke out in 1914, Bullard joined the French army. He fought in some of the bloodiest battles of the war, including one at Verdun, France, where he was wounded.

After recovering, Bullard joined the French Air Service, where he learned how to fly. He flew more than 20 missions. When the United States entered the war, American-born flyers were invited to join the US Air Service. Bullard, who had received numerous medals for bravery from the French, applied. His request was ignored. Only whites were accepted into the US Air Service at the time. Bullard died in 1961. In 1994, he was posthumously promoted to the rank of second lieutenant in the US Air Force in recognition of his courage in battle.

Lafayette Escadrille, an air squadron mostly made up of volunteer US flyers. The Americans quickly learned how to fly some of the most advanced French-made airplanes. Under the command of French Captain Georges Thenault, the unit shot down 57 enemy planes while fighting for the Allied cause in World War I. The knowledge these pilots gained while serving in France later advanced aviation in the United States.

The United States entered World War I on April 6, 1917. The air war was in full swing by that time. The US military owned about 250 airplanes, but none were combat ready. To fill the gap, the United States purchased fighter planes from France and the United Kingdom.

While the United States sent more than 2 million ground troops into battle in World War I, the men in open-cockpit biplanes grabbed much of the glory. Courageous US fighter pilots such as Eddie Rickenbacker and Frank Luke became heroes. Their breathtaking exploits, along with those of other American flyers, turned these elite airmen into legends and showed how trained pilots with first-rate airplanes could contribute to a war effort.

The commanders of Allied aerial forces captured headlines by using airstrikes to turn the tide of the war. One of them, US Army Brigadier General William "Billy" Mitchell, orchestrated a major air offensive at Saint-Mihiel

Many aircraft of World War I had two or three wings, features that generate extra lift but limit a plane's top speed.

ACES

Eddie Rickenbacker and Frank Luke both received the Congressional Medal of Honor for their efforts in World War I. They were among the nation's top aces. An ace is a pilot who shoots down five or more enemy aircraft during combat.

Rickenbacker was a race car driver in civilian life. He enlisted in the US Army in 1917, shortly after the United States entered World War I. By the time the war ended, Rickenbacker was the United States' best fighter pilot, having shot down 26 enemy aircraft.

Luke was credited with 18 aerial victories in the span of ten missions.[4] Wounded by enemy fire on September 29, 1918, he managed to land his plane but died of his wounds a short time later. He was 21 years old.

The top ace of the war was Manfred von Richthofen of Germany. Nicknamed "the Red Baron," he shot down approximately 80 planes before being shot down himself in April 1918.[5]

in northeastern France. The attack proved an air force could have a direct impact on a ground battle. With the Germans entrenched in Saint-Mihiel, the United States sent 600,000 ground troops on September 12, 1918, to destroy the enemy stronghold.[3]

Soon before the ground troops arrived, Mitchell devised a plan to hammer German troops from the air. The general had under his command nearly 1,500 planes from a coalition of Allied nations, and he used all of them. His aircraft relentlessly bombed the enemy from all sides. The massive aerial attack cut off German supply routes, prevented reinforcements from reaching the battlefield, and overwhelmed German airpower. Within a few days, 16,000 Germans surrendered and Saint-Mihiel was in Allied hands. In November, the combatants signed an armistice, ending the war with

After the war, US ace Eddie Rickenbacker provided his consulting services to the military and ran an airline company.

an Allied victory. A well-executed air attack had a hand in determining the outcome of the war. Airpower was coming into prominence as a key part of nations' militaries.

CHAPTER THREE
EARNING THEIR WINGS

When World War I ended on November 11, 1918, General Mitchell returned to the United States as a popular war hero with a cause. He wanted to make the air service an independent branch of the nation's armed services, alongside the army and the navy. At this point, the air service was still part of the army.

Mitchell's predictions about the importance of military aviation would be proven right less than 20 years after the war's end.

Few in the military or the US government agreed with Mitchell. In fact, after the war, cutbacks were made in the air service, reducing both personnel and equipment. Mitchell became outspoken during the early 1920s about the country's need to increase its airpower. He publicly criticized his superiors in the army for not bolstering the nation's air forces.

Mitchell saw the airplane as a weapon better able to protect the United States than a battleship. In October 1923, the army sent Mitchell on a fact-finding tour to the Pacific Ocean. He studied the US defenses in the area, visiting Hawaii, the Philippines, the Marianas, and Japan. Upon his return, Mitchell presented the War Department with a written account of his findings, along with some alarming conclusions. He reported that Pearl Harbor, the site of a US naval base in Hawaii, was practically defenseless. He saw a lack of cooperation at the base

The base at Pearl Harbor was a major center of US power in the Pacific.

between the army and the navy. He wrote that the growing Japanese military could easily attack Pearl Harbor from the air. He felt the United States had to not only match but also exceed the output of the Japanese aviation industry.

The US War Department filed his report away and forgot about it. Mitchell, however, kept hammering away, airing his disagreements with the government. His criticisms of the nation's top military leaders became so inflammatory that President Calvin Coolidge ordered Mitchell court-martialed in late September 1925 on the charge of insubordination. After he was found guilty, Mitchell resigned from the army. In civilian life, Mitchell continued his campaign for more military airpower until his death in 1936.

CHANGES ON THE HORIZON

By the 1930s, changes were coming in the aircraft industry, mainly because European nations and Japan had been developing their air forces since the end of World War I. Gone were the once-popular biplanes with their fragile wooden frames and cloth skin. All-metal monoplanes with enclosed cockpits now populated the skies.

The world political scene was changing as well. In September 1931, Japan invaded the Chinese province of Manchuria. The Japanese continued taking over parts of China. By 1933, military leaders in the United States realized Japan was preparing to expand its military reach into the Pacific Ocean.

In Germany, meanwhile, the Nazi Party came to power in July 1932. Adolf Hitler became Germany's chancellor six months later. Germany made no secret it was gearing up for another war. Both Germany and Japan were building strong air forces.

In response, the US Congress began budgeting money to substantially increase the number of aircraft the US Army could purchase. The additional funds also allowed the air force, now known as the US Army Air Corps (USAAC), to add more pilots and ground crew members. US General Henry "Hap" Arnold took command of the USAAC on September 29, 1938. Arnold had served with Mitchell and favored a strong air force. He pushed for research and the development of new aircraft, including the B-17 Flying Fortress and B-24 Liberator long-range bombers. He oversaw the introduction of sleek new fighter planes as well, including the twin-engine P-38 Lightning. He worked tirelessly to prepare the USAAC for war in Europe and the Pacific.

WORLD WAR II

When Germany invaded Poland on September 1, 1939, World War II (1939–1945) was officially underway. That

Arnold had been one of the first military pilots trained by the Wright brothers.

invasion prompted the Allies, led by France and the United Kingdom, to declare war on Germany. In 1940, Germany signed a pact with Italy and Japan, establishing the three nations as the Axis powers. Meanwhile, the United States stayed out of the war and kept building up its airpower.

It also renamed the USAAC to the United States Army Air Forces (USAAF) on June 20, 1941.

On December 7, 1941, Japan bombed the US Navy base at Pearl Harbor in Hawaii. The surprise attack left more than 2,000 Americans dead and destroyed dozens of USAAF and navy aircraft and ships.[1] The day after the attack, the United States declared war on Japan. Germany then declared war on the United States.

The USAAF played a significant role in bringing the war to an end four years later. Crucial to ending the hostilities was the destruction of Germany's munitions factories. USAAF bombers relentlessly went after those targets, dodging German artillery fire and fighter planes. Aircraft of the USAAF also joined forces with planes from the United Kingdom to carry out the Combined Bomber Offensive, a bombing campaign that attacked rocket launching sites, oil production facilities, and rail yards. The air force also conducted bombing raids in advance of Allied ground troops' attacks on German strongholds. They flew paratroopers behind enemy lines and brought valuable supplies to troops embroiled in battle. The P-51 Mustang emerged as one of the most dominant US fighter planes of the war. Massive raids by B-17, B-24, and B-25 bombers crippled German industry. The B-25 was known as the Mitchell; it was named after General Billy Mitchell in recognition of his passionate advocacy for airpower.

The B-25 was known as a rugged aircraft that could take damage and continue flying.

In the Pacific, the USAAF carried out the first bombing campaign against mainland Japan on April 18, 1942. At a time in the war when the momentum was still with the Japanese forces, US Navy aircraft carriers carried 16 B-25 bombers, which were normally based on land, within striking distance of Japan.[2] They dropped bombs on Japan's capital, Tokyo, among other targets, before running out of fuel and crash-landing in the Soviet Union and China. Most of the pilots and crew survived and eventually returned home. The raid, led by Lieutenant Colonel James Doolittle, caused relatively little damage to Japan but boosted morale on the home front. As the United States began advancing on Japan in the ensuing months and years, bombing missions against Japanese territory intensified. The USAAF's Fifth Air Force, led by George Kenney, provided air cover for forces in the South Pacific. By 1945, hundreds of bombers filled the skies during raids on Tokyo and other major Japanese cities. Using special bombs designed to ignite fires, they destroyed huge portions of the urban areas they attacked. Japanese buildings, largely constructed from wood, burned easily.

After Germany surrendered on May 8, 1945, fighting continued in the Pacific. In August, B-29 Superfortress bombers dropped atomic bombs on the Japanese cities of Hiroshima and Nagasaki. Japan agreed to surrender on August 15, 1945, ending World War II. More than 40,000 members of the USAAF had died during the war. The contributions of the USAAF were immense.

The Strategic Air Command (SAC), responsible for the nation's nuclear force, was created in March 1946. It controlled the air force bombers and missiles that

VINDICATION

Many of Mitchell's predictions came true, including the bombing of Pearl Harbor by the Japanese, the need for a strong air force, and the role airpower would play in future wars. Mitchell did not live to see the US Air Force established as an independent branch of the military. In 1942, six years after his death, President Franklin D. Roosevelt posthumously promoted Mitchell to the rank of major general. Mitchell was awarded the Congressional Medal of Honor posthumously by the US Congress in 1946. He is considered the father of the US Air Force.

would be used to deliver nuclear weapons in the event of a war.

On July 26, 1947, President Harry Truman signed the National Security Act into law. When the law took effect on September 18, it restructured the nation's military. Part of this restructuring made the United States Air Force a separate branch of the US armed forces. Airpower has been important in all US military conflicts since the air force became an independent branch of the US armed services. It would see a major test only a few years after its inception, during the Korean War (1950–1953).

THE BERLIN AIRLIFT

The air force would be tested soon after World War II. The Soviet Union and the United States had been allies during the war, but tensions escalated between them almost immediately afterward. Berlin, Germany's capital, was occupied by both nations and was at the center of these tensions. In June 1948, the Soviets blocked road, rail, and water routes to the parts of Berlin under US control. The blockade prevented food and supplies from getting to the people living in those areas of the city. The US Air Force organized a massive relief effort, known as the Berlin Airlift.

Over the next several months, the US Air Force, along with the air forces of the United Kingdom, Australia, New Zealand, and South Africa, made nearly 300,000 flights to Berlin, delivering crates of food, fuel, and other necessities.[3] The success of the airlift eventually led to the lifting of the Soviet blockade in May 1949. The Berlin Airlift led to the official separation of East Germany and West Germany into separate nations. The East was aligned with the Soviet Union, and the West was aligned with the United States. Berlin itself was similarly split down the middle.

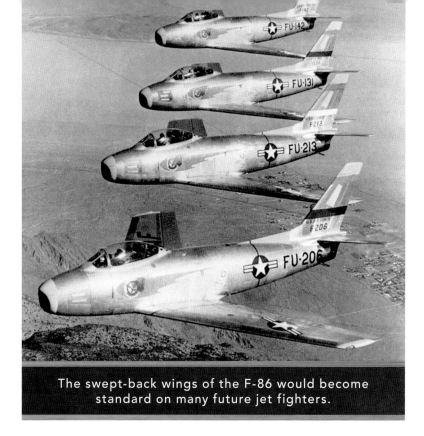

The swept-back wings of the F-86 would become standard on many future jet fighters.

KOREA AND VIETNAM

When North Korean troops invaded South Korea on June 25, 1950, one of the first responses came from the US Air Force. The North Koreans, backed by the Soviet Union and China, were armed with tanks, artillery, and combat planes.

In the early days of the war, as North Korean troops advanced on the South Korean capital of Seoul, US Air Force planes mounted a defense of the city. They bombed advancing enemy troops, destroyed tanks, cut off routes to the city, and attacked North Korean supply lines. That gave the United States time to prepare its ground troops to enter the war. The war went on until July 27, 1953.

During the conflict, the air force bombed industrial sites in North Korean cities. Jet fighter planes saw widespread use for the first time in combat. US pilots in F-86 Sabre jets fought Soviet MiG fighter jets sent to support North Korea.

The US Air Force served in much the same capacity during the Vietnam War (1959–1975), defending South Vietnam from North Vietnamese troops. The air force led the way in Operation Rolling Thunder, a sustained bombardment of North Vietnam that went on for more than three years beginning in 1965. It became one of the most intense air battles ever conducted by the United States.

THE COLD WAR

Both the Korean War and the Vietnam War took place during a period known as the Cold War. This was a time of extreme military and political tension between the United States and the Soviet Union. The two countries were divided by ideology, with the democratic United States facing off against the Communist Soviet Union. What made the Cold War distinct from other wars was that the two principal nations never directly clashed with each other. Instead, they engaged each other militarily in so-called proxy wars by supporting opposing sides in countries such as Korea and Vietnam.

CHAPTER FOUR

HIGH-TECH AIRPOWER

Iraqi President Saddam Hussein's order for his troops to invade Kuwait on August 2, 1990, marked the beginning of the Persian Gulf War (1990–1991). In response, on August 7, the US Air Force launched Operation Desert Shield. Within five days of the invasion, the US Air Force had substantial air and ground forces ready for combat.

The Iraqi military set fire to Kuwait's oil wells during its retreat.

The United Nations (UN) Security Council worked for months to find a peaceful resolution to the conflict. When those efforts failed, a UN coalition force, led by the United States, took military action on January 17, 1991. A hard-hitting aerial assault that lasted nearly a month and a half, followed by a four-day ground war, finally put an end to the Iraqi occupation of Kuwait. A precision air attack, with the US Air Force flying most of the sorties, left Iraq reeling. The US Air Force led an aerial bombardment of Iraq that took out radar sites, missile launch areas, communication centers, command bunkers, weapons production facilities, and airfields. The air attack broke the back of the Iraqi military and brought a quick end to the conflict. By the end of the war, approximately 20,000 Iraqi and 300 coalition soldiers were dead. Approximately 2,300 Iraqi civilians had died.[1] The US Air Force had flown more than 65,000 missions in the span of less than two months.[2]

SPACE SYSTEMS

The range of weapons employed by the US Air Force in the Persian Gulf War was unparalleled. It set the stage for the weaponry used in the War in Afghanistan (2001–present) and the Iraq War (2003–2011). Airmen showed their expertise in using a wide range of military hardware. One class of this hardware does not fire weapons at all, yet it is among the most important elements of the US arsenal. A constellation of satellites helps provide critical intelligence to the US military. These systems are run by the US Air Force.

One of the stars of the Gulf War still in use today is the Air Force Defense Support Program (DSP), which operates a series of reconnaissance satellites that serves as

The DMSP satellites use solar panels to power themselves.

an early warning system. The US Air Force used the DSP throughout the Gulf War to detect missile launches against coalition forces. This gave coalition troops warnings in advance of attacks. The system has undergone five major upgrades since its inception in 1970, the latest coming in December 2007.

In addition, the Defense Meteorological Satellite Program (DMSP) played a key role in predicting weather patterns during the aerial assault over Iraq in 1991. The information was vital because the area was experiencing rapidly changing weather. The DMSP became just as crucial in the War in Afghanistan. The system has been operational for more than 40 years, providing high-quality weather information to US and allied military units around the world.

The air force also relies heavily on the Defense Satellite Communications System (DSCS) for secure voice and data communication among forces on land, in the air, and on the seas. Considered the workhorse of the military satellite communications system, the DSCS is scheduled to be improved by a more advanced system called the Wide Band Global SATCOM System (WGS). Each WGS satellite has approximately ten times the capacity of the newest DSCS satellites.

One reason for the pinpoint accuracy of US air attacks in recent conflicts is the Global Positioning System (GPS). The system consists of dozens of satellites in orbit around Earth. They make it possible to identify exactly where something is on the surface of the planet. GPS allowed coalition air forces in the Gulf War to zero in on Iraqi missile positions, which were often hidden in urban areas. GPS is now widely used by civilians as well. Many smartphones use GPS signals for navigation.

At the heart of these complex systems are computers and sensors. It is the job of the US Air Force to keep these systems operational. The air force creates secure computer networks and tries to stay one step ahead of hackers who might attempt to cripple military operations by damaging those networks.

FIGHTERS

The flashiest aircraft in service with the US Air Force are its fighter jets. The most numerous is the compact, highly maneuverable F-16 Fighting Falcon. This reliable air-to-air combat plane can also be used in air-to-surface attacks. F-15s, including F-15 Eagles and F-15E Strike Eagles, are larger, faster, twin-engine fighters that can carry large loads of weapons. Combined, an F-15's engines can put out more thrust than the plane's weight. This means an F-15 can accelerate while flying straight up.

The air force's most advanced fighter is the F-22 Raptor. Unlike the fighters of the past, the F-22 is designed for stealth. It has a special shape and coatings designed to make it

THUNDERBIRDS

The F-16 Fighting Falcon is the current aircraft used by the legendary Thunderbirds, the demonstration squadron of the US Air Force. The squadron tours the world performing precision aerobatics. The Thunderbirds date back to 1953. The team has flown a variety of different aircraft through the years in shows that put the best of the US Air Force on display. There are 12 officers on the Thunderbird team, including the highly trained fighter pilots who fly in the shows.[3] More than 120 enlisted airmen, including mechanics and ground crews, are members of the Thunderbirds team as well.[4] The Thunderbirds have become an iconic part of the US Air Force. When the branch was honored on a postage stamp for its fiftieth anniversary in 1997, the Thunderbirds appeared on the stamp.

The F-22, *top*, and F-35, *bottom*, are among the most technologically advanced aircraft in the world.

nearly invisible to enemy radar. The mission of the F-22 is to shoot down enemy aircraft before they even know it is there. However, the F-22 is not just effective at a distance. It also has special features that make it highly maneuverable in close combat. Its engines are capable of thrust vectoring, meaning they can direct their power in different directions rather than only straight behind the aircraft. This lets the F-22 make tighter turns than most fighters its size.

The newest addition to the air force is the F-35 Lightning II. This fighter combines the stealth technology of the F-22 with the smaller size of the F-16. It is scheduled to enter service in mid-2016.

Just as important as the fighter jets are the weapons they carry. The AGM-65 Maverick, a guided missile directed against tanks and other armored military vehicles, has been carried by the F-15 and the F-16. The AGM-88 High-speed Anti-Radiation Missile (HARM) is an air-to-surface tactical missile designed to seek out and destroy enemy radar installations. The missiles have sensors that detect the transmissions sent out by these stations.

For air-to-air combat, US fighter jets use the AIM-120 Advanced Medium-Range Air-to-Air Missile (AMRAAM) and the AIM-9 Sidewinder. The AMRAAM locks on to enemy jets' radar and can be fired at a range of more than 30 miles (48 km).[5] The Sidewinder, a short-range missile in service since the 1950s, locks on to the heat given off by enemy aircraft.

BOMBERS AND ATTACKERS

US Air Force bomber and attack aircraft focus primarily on delivering crushing blows to ground targets. The B-52 Stratofortress is a long-range heavy bomber able to carry both conventional and nuclear weapons. It served as the backbone of the SAC's nuclear bomber force during the Cold War. The air force has been flying the B-52 for more than 50 years. The other key bombers in the US Air Force arsenal are the supersonic B-1 Lancer and the long-range stealth bomber known as the B-2 Spirit.

SMART BOMBS

The 1990s introduced a valuable new weapon to the air force arsenal—the Joint Direct Attack Munition (JDAM). This system is attached to normal bombs, converting them into guided bombs. It adds GPS equipment so the bomb knows exactly where it is. It also adds tail fins to the bomb, making it possible for the weapon to steer itself to a preset target. JDAMs, which have seen use in the War in Afghanistan, are programmed with the exact location of their target. Smoke or haze, which sometimes disrupt other targeting systems, do not interfere with the operation of JDAMs.

The A-10 Thunderbolt II is the key attack aircraft in service with the US Air Force. Smaller than a bomber, it is used for precision strikes in support of ground forces. This durable jet features the huge GAU-8 Avenger cannon. The seven-barrel gun fires large rounds at an incredible rate. It is capable of easily destroying tanks. The air force is considering retiring the A-10 in the mid-2010s. Another attack aircraft is the AC-130, a modified version of the C-130 cargo plane. The large plane flies wide, slow circles around a target, allowing its side-mounted cannons to continuously fire at the enemy.

OTHER AIRCRAFT

Fighters, bombers, and attack planes receive most of the public attention. But other US Air Force aircraft serve equally important roles. Cargo planes, helicopters, and drones are critical to the missions of today's air force.

Cargo planes deliver troops and equipment to faraway places in a matter of hours. The C-130 Hercules and C-17

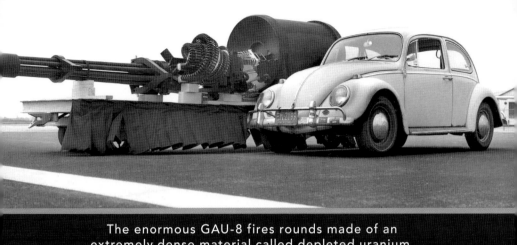

The enormous GAU-8 fires rounds made of an extremely dense material called depleted uranium, making it possible to destroy armored vehicles.

Globemaster III are among the air force's cargo aircraft. The HC-130, a special version of the C-130, carries fuel and can refuel other planes in midair. The enormous C-5 Galaxy is one of the largest airplanes in the world. It is the only plane that can carry any piece of the US Army's equipment, including heavy tanks.

Most helicopters in the US military belong to the army, but the air force also uses a few types. One is the HH-60 Pave Hawk, used primarily for evacuating wounded soldiers and troops trapped under heavy fire. The V-22 Osprey is similar to a helicopter and used for transport purposes. Its two huge propellers can face forward like those on an airplane or turn upward like those on a helicopter. It can even switch between these modes in midair. This means it can take off vertically while still achieving the range and speed of an airplane.

Unmanned aerial vehicles, commonly known as drones, are controlled remotely from the ground. They make it possible to carry out long-duration surveillance or attack missions without risking the lives of pilots. The MQ-1 Predator and the larger MQ-9 Reaper are among the most commonly used attack drones. The RQ-4 Global Hawk is used exclusively for surveillance purposes.

The advanced aircraft and weaponry used by the US Air Force give the branch enormous flexibility in carrying out its missions. Supported by the largest military budget in the world, the air force is determined to remain on the cutting edge of combat technology.

AIR FORCE ONE

Among the duties of the US Air Force is transporting the president of the United States. In 1943, the USAAF came up with the idea of a special plane for the president. Officials were concerned about the president flying on a regular aircraft with no special communications equipment or security. Today, special Boeing 747-200B passenger jets are modified and set aside for this purpose. Whenever the jets have the president aboard, they take on the name *Air Force One*. The planes can refuel in midair and are equipped with highly sophisticated, secure communications equipment. They even have a medical suite that can serve as an operating room. Since the president rarely travels alone, Air Force One has two kitchens that can prepare food to serve 100 people at a time.[6]

THE AIR FORCE'S BUDGET

FISCAL YEAR 2014

Operation and Maintenance	$46.577 billion
Personnel	$29.259 billion
Construction	$1.322 billion
Family Housing	$0.461 billion
Procurement	$18.837 billion
Research and Development	$17.561 billion
Base Realignment and Closures	$0.126 billion
Non-Discretionary Funding (including intelligence and health-care costs)	$30.280 billion
Total	$144.425 billion[7]

ARMED SERVICES BUDGET
FISCAL YEAR 2014

Army	$129.7 billion
Navy/Marines	$155.8 billion
Air Force	$144.4 billion
Coast Guard	$9.8 billion[8]

CHAPTER FIVE

THE AIR FORCE TODAY

Protecting US airspace and guarding the nation's interests around the world are enormous responsibilities. The US Air Force views its contribution to sustaining the nation's military advantage as a matter of 12 core functions.[1] These functions are interconnected,

The air force's upgrade programs mean that even older aircraft, such as the B-1 bomber, are equipped with the latest technology.

and the air force must succeed at all of them to remain at the cutting edge of military aviation.

The US Air Force's 12 core functions provide the framework for coordinating an effective plan for the nation's security. The core functions include: air superiority; global precision attack; global integrated intelligence, surveillance, and reconnaissance; cyberspace superiority; space superiority; nuclear deterrence operations; rapid global mobility; command and control; special operations; personnel recovery; agile combat support; and building partnerships.

Having air superiority allows the air force to deter and defeat any adversary it might face in the air. Controlling airspace over a battlefield enables other branches of the military to carry out their missions without enemy interference from the air. Ground and sea forces are

The air force uses both quality and quantity to achieve air superiority.

vulnerable to air attack, making this function of the air force critical.

The capability for a global precision attack means the air force must be able to strike a target anywhere in the world on the first try. Of all the branches of the military, the air force is the one that can respond to an act of aggression the fastest. Long-range aircraft and weaponry make this possible.

Global intelligence, surveillance, and reconnaissance (ISR) are crucial, even in times of peace. The aim is always to prevent an attack, whether it is from another country or a terrorist cell working independently. In battle, ISR becomes even more important. Integrating ISR across air, space, and cyberspace—and with all branches of the military—allows commanders to make informed decisions involving worldwide military operations. Using ISR, the air force has become a leader in combating global terrorism. Unmanned aerial vehicles have become vital tools in achieving this function.

Cyberspace has brought on a new wave of challenges in fighting a war. Communications and information networks are critically important in combat, but they are vulnerable to cyber attacks. By attaining cyberspace superiority, the air force foils those electronic invasions. Space superiority is a related function of the air force. Much of the military's communication and information technology relies on satellites, and protecting them is a mission of the air force. In addition, the air force is responsible for launching, operating, and maintaining satellites.

For more than 50 years, a strong and capable nuclear force has deterred nuclear war. It is the air force's job to manage the bombers and land-launched missiles that make up two-thirds of the nation's nuclear arsenal. The US Navy operates the submarine-launched missiles that make up the third part of the US nuclear force. Nuclear deterrence operations involve updating and maintaining the nation's nuclear weapons while working to prevent rogue nations from stockpiling their own nuclear weapons.

Rapid global mobility is a key part of the air force's mission. Because the US Air Force can get anywhere in the world quickly, the branch plays a vital role in giving aid to ground troops, evacuating casualties, making sure the wounded receive swift medical care, and bringing reinforcements to the battlefield. Recent military conflicts have involved coalitions of several nations, and the US Air Force has helped transport those forces to the battle scene. This function of the air force also involves delivering humanitarian relief supplies to disaster zones.

Coordinating different branches and units is key in today's military. In the air force, this is referred to as command and control. The air force makes sure commanders from all branches of the military are able

to communicate and monitor operations using secure networks. The North American Aerospace Defense Command, or NORAD, is a key component of this mission and is based near Colorado Springs, Colorado.

Because many military actions today center around counterterrorism, the role of special operations forces has grown substantially. These enemies cannot be fought using the same forces the military would use to fight a nation. Small, precise operations are most effective in capturing or killing terrorist leaders. Many of those operations count on forces from multiple branches of the military. The air force, besides having its own special operations units, is responsible for transporting special operations forces from other military branches to the scene of the mission.

Personnel recovery is critical during combat. Besides evacuating casualties from battle, the air force also conducts evacuations during disasters and carries out rescue operations when situations are too dangerous for other rescue workers to respond.

Not all of the air force's missions involve combat. It also supports airmen and their families. The air force offers a range of what it calls agile combat support services. These include the rehabilitation of wounded troops and quality-of-life services, such as health care, child care, and continuing education. Another noncombat objective of the air force is to build partnerships with foreign governments and military leaders in those

The air force helped Haitians evacuate after an earthquake struck their country in 2010.

countries. The goal is to forge solid working relationships with these friendly nations.

MAJOR COMMANDS

The air force is organized into ten major commands (MAJCOMs), each responsible for overseeing part of the US Air Force. Each command is further broken down into wings and then even smaller units called groups and squadrons. Each MAJCOM is headquartered at a particular air base.

Air Combat Command, based at Langley Air Force Base in Virginia, is the largest command and is responsible for providing air combat forces around the world. It operates bombers and fighter planes, as well as reconnaissance, rescue, cargo, and communications aircraft.

THE NATIONAL MUSEUM OF THE US AIR FORCE

Wright-Patterson Air Force Base in Ohio, the headquarters of the Air Force Materiel Command, is also the site of the National Museum of the United States Air Force. More than any other branch of the military, the US Air Force has worked extensively to preserve its history. Wright-Patterson Air Force Base is located just six miles (10 km) from Dayton, Ohio, the home of the Wright brothers.[2] The museum's three gigantic hangars house hundreds of historic aircraft and missiles. Included are examples of the F-15, F-16, F-22, and A-10. One notable aircraft is the B-29 named Bock's Car, which dropped an atomic bomb on the Japanese city of Nagasaki at the end of World War II.

Wright-Patterson Air Force Base in Ohio is the home of the Air Force Materiel Command. This command is in charge of research and development of all new weapons. It also handles purchasing, testing, and deploying these weapons. A separate command, the Air Force Global Strike Command, based at Barksdale Air Force Base in Louisiana, manages the nation's nuclear arsenal. Air force satellites are launched and maintained by the Air Force Space Command, based at Peterson Air Force Base in Colorado.

Air Mobility Command takes charge when troops and supplies are needed on the front lines or medical evacuations have to be made. It is headquartered at Scott Air Force Base in Illinois.

The smallest and most specialized of all the commands is the Air Force Special Operations Command. Located at Hurlburt Field in Florida, this elite group

SPECIAL FORCES

The US Air Force has several groups of special forces troops. Combat controllers enter dangerous, remote areas and direct air operations. They are experts in survival skills and are often skilled parachutists, divers, and motorcyclists. Pararescuemen jump out of aircraft behind enemy lines to rescue isolated soldiers and aircrews. Weather team specialists help coordinate the air force's planning with respect to potentially dangerous weather. Tactical air control party specialists move with army and marine units and are responsible for coordinating close air support for ground forces. Presently, all of these jobs are open only to males.

conducts the most sensitive missions in the air force. These missions are usually top secret and take place deep inside enemy lines.

The important job of recruiting and training airmen is handled by the Air Education and Training Command at Randolph Air Force Base in Texas. Additional personnel management is handled by the Air Force Reserve Command, which oversees the 125,000 reservists who serve in the US Air Force on a part-time basis. This command is located at Robins Air Force Base in Georgia.

US Air Force leaders met with the commander of the Royal Thai Air Force in 2010, one of many partnerships the air force fosters in the Pacific Ocean.

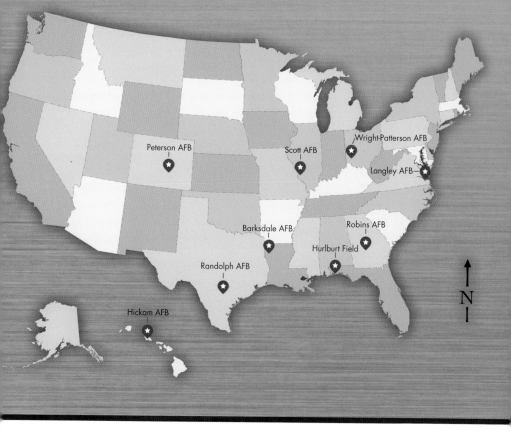

US AIR FORCE INSTALLATIONS IN THE UNITED STATES

Wright-Patterson AFB

Peterson AFB

Scott AFB

Langley AFB—

Barksdale AFB

Robins AFB

Hurlburt Field

Randolph AFB

Hickam AFB

N

US Air Forces in Europe works in Europe and Africa and is based at Ramstein Air Base in Germany. The Pacific Air Forces command is based at Hickam Field in Hawaii.

CHAPTER SIX
TEAMWORK

The US Air Force is known for sending fighters, bombers, and attack planes to provide air support for US troops and achieve air superiority. However, that is only part of the story of how the US Air Force contributes to the US military. Weather forecasters, air traffic controllers, and highly trained medical personnel are

among the specialists who make the air force the powerful, flexible force it has become.

Weather forecasting is rarely dangerous work, especially if the forecast is being made from behind a desk in a climate-controlled newsroom. But if the forecaster is an Air Force Special Operations weather technician

(SOWT) working in the eye of a swirling sandstorm or the middle of a rain-soaked, muddy battlefield with bullets flying overhead, weather forecasting becomes a job filled with risk.

SOWTs assist other branches of the US military in some of the most dangerous areas of the world. If Navy SEALs or Army Rangers are on a mission, there is a good chance an Air Force SOWT is working with them.

These special ops weather experts are both scientists and warriors. They go through the same rigorous training as all other members of the Air Force Special Operations units. That includes weapons, survival, and tactical training. In addition, those who want to serve in this prestigious unit must prove their skills as weather analysts during months of intensive training. They must be able to make atmospheric observations and

DROPPING IN

Sometimes a special operations weather technician will have to literally drop in to make a spur-of-the-moment, lifesaving weather assessment. A special operations army unit was on a mission in a valley in Afghanistan when a dense fog started to roll in. Weather patterns in Afghanistan are known to shift rapidly. Commanders wanted to evacuate the unit, but did not know if low-flying helicopters had enough time to get to the troops and fly out before the fog made it impossible to navigate safely. An air force special ops weatherman was immediately flown to the scene and parachuted down to the valley. He set up his equipment, analyzed the situation, and reported the helicopters had a one-hour window to airlift everyone out safely. The evacuation was carried out flawlessly.

precise climate-related calculations in places ranging from mountain peaks to sweltering jungles.

When they are in a war zone, these weather forecasters are prepared to respond if the enemy attacks. The work they do is vital. They might calculate exactly when a heavy rainstorm will strike, making it possible to plan a mission around the upcoming weather. They may gauge the flow and depth of a river to ensure it is safe for troops to cross.

Performing the specialized duties of an SOWT, including jumping from airplanes, requires a great deal of practice and training.

In regions such as Afghanistan, battles take place in mountainous terrain on a regular basis. Weather can wreak havoc on those trying to fly in helicopters to rescue the wounded. The information gathered by SOWTs lets commanders make decisions based on how the latest meteorological conditions will affect a mission.

Air Force Staff Sergeant Travis Sanford, a special ops weatherman, used his training in wind speed and direction, cloud conditions, and marksmanship to turn the tide of a battle during his first assignment with a US Marine Corps special operations team in Afghanistan on March 8, 2010. Just after sunrise, as the team was on a routine reconnaissance mission near a small Afghan village, they came under enemy fire. Sanford manned an M-249 light machine gun and, along with the rest of his team, engaged the insurgent fighters. A marine next to him suffered a gunshot wound to the head a few minutes after the battle began. Sanford, while under enemy heavy fire, administered first aid to the wounded soldier. Then, with the help of another marine, Sanford carried the wounded soldier toward a landing zone where he could be evacuated to a field hospital.

As bullets whizzed by him, Sanford collected the atmospheric data necessary for the approaching rescue helicopter to land so the crew could pick up the wounded

Combat controllers often operate in remote areas far from ordinary runways and airports.

marine. The SOWT then guided the helicopter safely as the battle raged on.

COMBAT FLIGHTS

Air force combat controllers are also familiar with high-stakes work. Their mission is to get airpower into a battle zone to support troops on the ground. Like SOWTs, combat controllers often serve in units made up of forces from other branches of the military.

It is the job of the combat controller to go into hostile territory undetected. Then, he needs to find a place to set up a landing strip for helicopters and planes and guide those aircraft in and out of the area. This is usually the only way other members of the US military can get into a combat zone or a disaster zone.

All combat controllers are certified air traffic controllers and in top physical condition. Oftentimes, a combat controller has to carry more than 100 pounds (45 kg) of equipment, including communication devices, lights, and laser target designators over miles of tough terrain.[1]

THE MEDICAL TEAM

In the heat of a long battle, when the critically injured need to be treated, the US Air Force will often fly in a special ops surgical and critical care team. The team includes surgeons, nurses, and technicians. The eight-person team is trained to set up anywhere and handle any medical crisis. They treat wounded soldiers and sometimes civilians.

The air force special ops surgical and critical care team stabilizes the wounded so they can be transported to a field hospital. The team works under the most difficult conditions with severe time pressure. Team members must bring along a supply of blood, intravenous fluids, anesthetics, ventilators, and other medical equipment. Many medical advances in US civilian trauma care units stem from how special ops teams respond to medical crises in a war zone.

CANINE SOLDIERS

Many military working dogs help the air force and other branches carry out their missions. All dogs serving in the US armed services are trained at Lackland Air Force Base in San Antonio, Texas. The US Air Force oversees the Military Working Dog Program for the Department of Defense. The 341st Training Squadron operates the program for the air force. The squadron trains both the dogs and their handlers. There are currently more than 2,700 dogs serving in the US military worldwide.[2]

The dogs are taught to sniff out bombs, track enemy troops, detect intruders, go on patrols, and handle search-and-rescue missions. The best breeds for military service are German shepherds and Belgian Malinois. When

GUARD DOG

Nemo, a German shepherd, graduated from training at Lackland Air Force Base. He served in Vietnam with his handler, Airman Robert Throneburg. In December 1966, the two were on patrol at night at an air base near Saigon, the capital of South Vietnam. Nemo heard enemy troops moving in the darkness at a nearby graveyard. They were trying to launch a surprise attack on the air base. Throneburg radioed for help, but was forced to start firing before reinforcements arrived. The airman shot two of the invaders but was wounded himself. Nemo went after the enemy to keep them away from his handler. Flashing his sharp teeth, Nemo fearlessly lunged at the oncoming enemy commandos. They turned and ran, but not before they shot the dog in the eye and nose. Nemo kept going and, once certain the invaders were gone for good, he rushed back to his handler and covered the wounded man's body until help arrived. Both Throneburg and Nemo survived their injuries. The brave canine was retired and lived at Lackland Air Base until his death in 1972.

Like their human counterparts, military working dogs wear identification tags around their necks.

the dogs reach seven months of age, members of the 341st Squadron begin teaching them the skills needed to serve the nation in combat.

The dogs save human lives. With their sensitive noses, they are able to detect bombs much faster than humans and alert their handlers. Prospective military dogs undergo an intensive 120-day training program, where they are taught basic obedience and some advanced skills, such as sniffing out various dangerous substances. If the dogs make it through the initial training, they go on to more difficult tasks and learn to work as a team with a handler. Not every dog makes it through the initial training session, and even some of those that do are not chosen for military service. The Military Working Dog program is very selective. Like their human counterparts, the dogs must have the right personality and disposition to serve in the armed forces.

CHAPTER SEVEN
CAREERS IN THE AIR FORCE

J ust as in civilian life, there is a wide range of careers
in the US Air Force. While some of those careers
are spent in the cockpit of a fighter plane or bomber,
most are on the ground. All require different skills and
talents. These jobs tap into a person's interests and
area of expertise. Members of the air force are divided

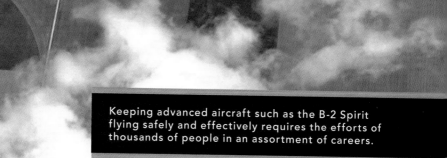

Keeping advanced aircraft such as the B-2 Spirit flying safely and effectively requires the efforts of thousands of people in an assortment of careers.

into two main groups: officers and enlisted personnel. Officers include pilots, lawyers, doctors, and other people with advanced training or degrees. Enlisted personnel generally have less responsibility, but their jobs are critical to the strength of the air force. For enlisted personnel, there are four job categories: administrative, mechanical, electronics, and general. Each category includes many varied jobs. Wherever they work, members of the US Air Force are dedicated to making sure the branch maintains its edge in air combat.

ADMINISTRATIVE CAREERS

As in any big organization, many people work behind the scenes doing administrative tasks to keep the US Air Force running smoothly. In the air force, administrative assignments involve much more than just paperwork. Some airmen are in charge of maintaining the personnel files for the vast number of people serving in the branch. Other administrative careers include managing finances, airfields, and supplies.

Logistics is another administrative career option in the air force. Planning is the key to any successful military operation, and the airmen who handle logistics are tasked with drawing up these plans. The US Air Force has a plan for just about every possible event, and if something unforeseen happens, a plan has to be quickly developed to handle that crisis.

Traffic management specialists are also part of the air force administrative team. This is a very important position, considering the air force has billions of dollars worth of equipment and supplies. Keeping track of the location of this equipment throughout the world at any given time is the complex task of these specialists.

MECHANICAL CAREERS

Those who opt for mechanical careers in the air force work with some of the most complex and sophisticated equipment ever invented. There are jobs available in aircraft electric systems, aircraft ejection systems, aircraft metals technology, and missile and space systems maintenance.

Other careers in this category include aircrew flight equipment specialists. These aircrews are responsible for making sure all the emergency equipment in every aircraft the air force deploys works flawlessly. From parachutes to survival kits, in an emergency this equipment can mean the difference between life and death for aircrews and pilots.

FEMALE FLIERS

Nearly 19 percent of US Air Force members are women.[1] At one time women were not allowed to fly for their nation's armed services in combat. Still, an intrepid group of women fliers came forward in World War II to help the US Army Air Forces with urgent needs. The Women Airforce Service Pilots (WASPs) flew new planes—more than 12,000 in all—from factories to air bases all over the country.[2] This freed up male pilots to fly combat missions. When Congress passed the Women's Armed Forces Integration Act in 1948, women began signing up for air force duty. But they were assigned mostly to handle clerical jobs and were not allowed to become pilots until 1976. Even then, women were not permitted to fly combat missions until 1993. Today women—both enlisted and officers—hold down nearly all job types in the air force. The only exceptions are in some special forces units.

There is hardly a more important job on the ground to a pilot than the aerospace maintenance specialist. Keeping air force aircraft in perfect working order is a key priority for these specialists. It is up to aerospace maintenance specialists to inspect each plane and, if something is broken, repair it immediately or take the aircraft out of service. Without them, planes would not even make it off the ground.

Another important career in the mechanical field is that of air traffic control operations specialists. In this career, airmen handle air traffic flow with an eye toward keeping everyone who flies into their airspace safe. They are also trained to aid aircraft in emergency situations.

ELECTRONICS CAREERS

Arming aircraft, transmitting radio signals, and operating radar and weapon systems all come down to electronics, which is one of the most important careers in the US Air Force. A dedicated group of airmen makes sure these systems remain in working order.

Among those working in air force electronics careers are avionics test and components specialists, who maintain the flight control, flight data recorder, communication, and radar systems in air force aircraft. These specialists test the various electronic systems on a

Airmen who work with electronics and radar are often responsible for tracking many streams of information at once.

plane, ensuring they are calibrated correctly and working properly. They also make any needed repairs.

Ground radar systems specialists install, maintain, and repair air traffic control, warning radar, and weather systems. Sensor operator specialists are also on the air force electronics staff. Also known as drone operators, these specialists work in surveillance and reconnaissance. They provide real-time battle damage assessments and use precision-guided weapons to knock out targets.

GENERAL CAREERS

The general category encompasses a wide range of careers, from medical services in laboratories, clinics, emergency rooms, and pharmacies to fire protection, base security, engineering, imagery analysis, and jobs that require computer skills, such as communications.

Paralegal specialists fall under the general career category. The air force has an active legal department, known as the Judge Advocate General's Corps. Paralegals juggle a variety of tasks, including doing legal research in multiple areas of the law and conducting accident investigations.

Getting the story of today's air force out to a global audience is the job of public affairs specialists. Writing news and feature stories for print, digital, radio, television, and social media helps keep the

THE AIR FORCE CIVILIAN SERVICE

There are more than 190,000 civilians working for the US Air Force around the world.[3] Nearly 170,000 are US citizens; the others are foreign citizens employed at air bases overseas.[4] Civilian employees hold down many different types of jobs in the air force. They support the men and women on active duty in the air force and are dedicated to the same goals of protecting liberty and freedom as their military counterparts. There is a broad spectrum of civilian jobs, including engineers, teachers, scientists, environmental professionals, computer technicians, mechanics, health professionals, and many more. The jobs offer salaries and benefits competitive with comparable jobs in the private sector. Civilian employees have no military obligation and do not wear uniforms.

public informed about the work that is going on at US Air Force bases around the world.

There are also jobs for cryptologic linguists. This career focuses on translating foreign communications for intelligence purposes. The air force is always on the lookout for those with a knack for foreign languages, including Farsi, Russian, Pashto, and Korean, just to name a few.

Explosive ordnance disposal, another career in this category, is not a job for the faint of heart. These specialists are trained to locate and disarm explosive devices of all kinds, including radioactive, chemical, and biological bombs. Airmen in this line of work are part of base emergency response teams.

PROTECTING CYBERSPACE

One of the biggest job growth areas in the US Air Force is in protecting cyberspace. As the military's dependence on computers, networks, and information technology grows at an ever-increasing pace, so does the risk of damage from destructive hacking. Attacks on federal agency computers are extremely common, with approximately 50,000 incidents reported in 2012 alone.[5] Cyberwarriors in the US Air Force protect national security by defending the nation's computer and information systems and attacking hackers trying to penetrate these networks.

CAREERS FOR OFFICERS

Officers also have numerous career choices in the air force. These jobs have greater responsibility than the jobs carried out by enlisted personnel,

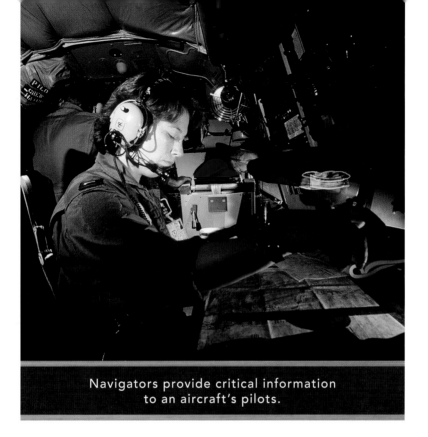

Navigators provide critical information to an aircraft's pilots.

a difference reflected in the pay scale. Notably, only officers can pilot aircraft. Careers are divided into four categories: flight, technical, nontechnical, and specialty.

There are several different types of pilots: bomber pilots, tanker pilots, fighter pilots, test pilots, and helicopter pilots, among others. Flight careers also encompass combat systems officers and air battle managers. Navigators guide a military aircraft where it needs to go and target and fire missiles and bombs. These members of the flight crew make it possible for the pilot to focus on flying the plane rather than switching tasks. Air battle managers make split-second decisions during air combat. They plan and coordinate air operations, even deciding which planes to use. They must be knowledgeable about all aircraft and weapon systems.

Officers in technical careers include mechanical, civil, and aerospace engineers. Scientists and weather officers are found in this field as well. Also included in this category are acquisition managers, who plan for and obtain equipment and supplies.

SPECIAL TRAINING

Civilian doctors, lawyers, nurses, chaplains, and others who seek specialty careers must go through Commissioned Officer Training, which is basic training for professionals in these fields who enter the air force. The training is a five-week program.[6] It is divided into physical fitness, leadership, and academic courses. It is an introduction to military life and teaches these professionals about the air force way of doing things, including the importance of taking and giving orders.

Both technical and nontechnical officers hold leadership positions. Many nontechnical officers are administrators and managers in fields such as security forces, communications, and logistics. Intelligence gathering is another nontechnical field. In this position an officer is involved in gathering information about the enemy while at the same time safeguarding air force information networks. Intelligence officers

Chaplains in the US Air Force often help with the branch's humanitarian missions around the world.

analyze the information collected and assess an adversary's strengths and weaknesses.

Lawyers, doctors, nurses, dentists, and veterinarians are some of the specialty careers filled by officers. These officers must be licensed to practice in their chosen fields when they join the air force. Chaplains are also members of the specialty career field. They provide professional religious support to airmen of all faiths.

CHAPTER EIGHT

LIFE IN THE AIR FORCE

Becoming a member of the US Air Force is no simple task. The air force seeks out recruits who have the skills to work on aircraft and other complex equipment. Each prospective candidate for the air force must be in top physical condition and between the ages of 18—or 17, with parental consent—and 27. Applicants must be

Entering the US Air Force Academy is one of several ways to join the air force.

US citizens or legal, permanent residents. They must also have a high school diploma. In addition, those who want to enlist in the US Air Force have to take the Armed Services Vocational Aptitude Battery (ASVAB) test. Though the ASVAB evaluates candidates in a variety of subjects, there is a heavy emphasis on math and science. Mechanical comprehension is another key aspect of the test.

Each branch of the military sets its own score a prospective recruit has to attain to be accepted for service. The score needed to enter the air force is one of the highest. The ASVAB is also used to determine which jobs are best suited for a particular enlistee.

New recruits are usually matched up with a series of jobs and given a choice as to which job they would like. The air force makes the ultimate decision based on how many people are needed in each area. Before any job assignments are given out, those who are accepted into the US Air Force undergo basic training at Lackland Air Force Base in Texas.

Basic training is an 8.5-week course in which enlistees are challenged both physically and mentally. They are taught to be warriors, but they also learn survival strategies and combat first aid. Recruits are taught how to deal with biological, chemical, and nuclear threats. They increase their physical endurance and become mentally prepared for combat and leadership.

When basic training is completed, airmen are given their orders and sent to various bases to begin their technical training. Education is a big part of air force life, and continuing education is stressed. In the high-tech world of the US Air Force, airmen take courses in electronics, information technology, logistics,

Basic training involves obstacle courses that test enlistees' physical abilities.

metals technology, telecommunications, and aircraft maintenance, among other subjects.

The courses are offered at the many campuses of the Community College of the Air Force. These college-level courses can eventually lead to an associate's degree.

TAKING THE ROTC ROUTE

Those who decide to enter the air force by joining the AFROTC take a number of air force–related courses alongside their regular college classes. The military courses include subjects such as air force structure and the history of air power. AFROTC cadets also participate in leadership training that hones their skills as military leaders and teaches air force protocol. Cadets who are in the AFROTC program go to basic training the summer between their sophomore and junior years of college and must complete it successfully before continuing with the program. Once they graduate from college and the AFROTC program, cadets are commissioned second lieutenants. AFROTC cadets must commit to serving in the air force for four years of active duty and four years of inactive duty.

Enlisted airmen can reach the rank of chief master sergeant. To become a commissioned officer, the air force requires a four-year degree.

ENTERING AS AN OFFICER

There are three ways to join the air force as an officer. Many people join the Air Force Reserve Officer Training Corps (AFROTC) at the college they attend. There are 144 colleges with AFROTC detachments on campus.[1] Those interested in entering AFROTC must pass a physical examination. An air force officer must also interview them. The AFROTC offers scholarships and pays full or partial tuition for those in the program. Members of the AFROTC complete military training while continuing to work toward their college degrees. Priority is often given to those majoring in a technical or scientific field.

Attending the United States Air Force Academy in Colorado Springs, Colorado, is another way to enter the air force as a commissioned officer. The Air Force Academy is one of the top educational institutions in the country. It is difficult to get into the Air Force Academy; only approximately ten percent of the students who apply each year get accepted.[2] Both men and women can attend the college. Women were first admitted in 1976. Those entering the academy must make it through five weeks of Basic Cadet Training, an introduction to military life, before starting classes at the academy.[3]

The US Air Force Academy's iconic chapel was completed in 1963.

GETTING THE NOD

The chance of getting into the United States Air Force Academy is greatly enhanced if a candidate is nominated for admission by a member of Congress or the vice-president of the United States. Candidates with outstanding grades in high school who want to go to the Air Force Academy should make their interest known to elected federal officials well in advance of their application. In some areas of the country, competition for these nominations is stiff, and elected officials have a limited number of nominations they can make each year.

Cadets attending the Air Force Academy are offered more than 30 college majors, along with athletic conditioning and military training. Based on the needs of the air force, the four-year program puts a heavy emphasis on science, engineering, and military studies. Tuition and all expenses are paid for those who attend the school; in return, cadets make a five-year commitment to active duty. Cadets graduate from the Air Force Academy at the rank of second lieutenant.

The third way to enter the US Air Force as a commissioned officer is by attending Officer Training School at Maxwell Air Force Base in Alabama after graduating from college with a four-year degree. The tough nine-week program provides both military and leadership training. Physical fitness and problem solving are stressed in this intensive course.

Anyone who wants to become an officer in the US Air Force must pass an exam called the Air Force

A DAY AT THE UNITED STATES AIR FORCE ACADEMY

As each day dawns at the US Air Force Academy, cadets are reminded of the school's core values: "Integrity first, Service before self, Excellence in all we do."[4]

Unlike at most colleges, days at the academy are highly organized and well planned. Cadets wake up at 5:00 a.m. and by 5:15 they begin detail, which involves taking care of chores around campus such as cleaning bathrooms and collecting garbage. Breakfast is at 7:00, and all cadets eat together at the same time.

Classwork starts at 7:30; there are four classes lasting 53 minutes each. Students attend classes in uniform. Lunch begins at noon. Cadets usually have 30 minutes to eat. Classes resume at 12:30 p.m., and the afternoon session features three 55-minute classes. At 4:00 students can participate in extracurricular activities, such as sports or clubs. Dinner is served at 6:00. Cadets study between the hours of 7:00 and 11:00. The lights are turned off at 11 p.m. Air force cadets are expected to accomplish a variety of tasks each day and do them well. The structure at the Air Force Academy is designed so cadets learn how to manage their time efficiently, give priority to what needs to be done, and accomplish their goals before moving on to the next undertaking.

Officer Qualifying Test. It evaluates students' language, math, science, and basic aviation knowledge. It also tests students' ability to think about and visualize three-dimensional objects. Officers are placed in a number of positions in the air force, including handling battle management and serving as pilots and combat systems officers.

Those who want to become pilots or combat systems officers must make a major commitment to the air force. This is because of the amount of specialized training the air force puts into developing outstanding aircrews. Pilots must complete an approximately one-year training course and agree to stay in the air force for ten years. Combat systems officers must commit to six years of service.

BENEFITS

As with civilian careers, serving in the air force is a job with pay and benefits. Officers make more money than enlisted airmen. The salary for an enlisted member of the air force

ACADEMY EXTRAS

Like most colleges, the US Air Force Academy offers plenty of extracurricular activities. The academy participates in a number of intercollegiate sports, including football, baseball, basketball, track and field, and soccer. There are intramural sports teams as well. One of the most daring activities is the academy parachuting team, called Wings of Blue. Few earn a spot on this elite squad. Other clubs include karate, judo, and mountaineering. The school's mascot is a falcon, chosen because of the bird's courage and power.

ranges from approximately $18,000 a year for an airman basic to $88,000 for a chief master sergeant with more than 40 years of experience.[5] But there are bonuses for more stressful jobs, hazardous duty, and urgently needed positions. The pay scale for officers ranges from

One benefit of air force service is the opportunity to have extreme experiences found nowhere else.

approximately $34,000 for second lieutenants to $230,000 for generals.[6]

Benefits for all air force members include free medical and dental care, an opportunity to buy relatively inexpensive life insurance, and 30 days' paid vacation per year. A retirement package is available after 20 years.[7]

While most members of the US Air Force live on an air base, some live off base. A tax-free allowance is given to those who reside off base to help cover the cost of rent or mortgage payments. Single airmen can live in free dormitory-style rooms on base. For air force personnel with families, there are free single-family houses on base.

There are plenty of leisure and recreational opportunities on air force bases, including gyms, swimming pools, bowling alleys, and camping facilities. When they are not working, airmen can go to school or get involved in volunteer community activities near the base. Wherever air force personnel live, and whatever their specific duties, they are sure to experience things that are rare or impossible in civilian life. From the cockpit of a stealth fighter to the remote deserts of Afghanistan to the glow of a satellite control center, members of the US Air Force work to keep the world's skies safe.

AIR FORCE RANKS

Enlisted

Enlisted
Airman Basic
<------------------- Airman
Airman First Class
Senior Airman
Staff Sergeant
Technical Sergeant
Master Sergeant
Senior Master Sergeant
Chief Master Sergeant -------->
Chief Master Sergeant of the Air Force

Officers

Officers
Second Lieutenant
First Lieutenant
<------------------- Captain
Major
Lieutenant Colonel ---------->
Colonel
Brigadier General
Major General
Lieutenant General
<------------------- General

TIMELINE

1903

The Wright brothers successfully test a heavier-than-air flying machine on December 17.

1908

On February 10, the Wright brothers reach an agreement to sell a Wright Military Flyer to the US government.

1917

On April 6, the United States enters World War I to help the Allied powers with troops and pilots.

1938

US General Henry "Hap" Arnold, architect of the US Air Force, takes command of the US Army Air Corps on September 29.

1941

On December 8, the United States enters World War II. The US Army Air Forces play a major role in the conflict.

1946

The Strategic Air Command is established in March.

1947

The US Air Force becomes an independent branch of the US military on September 18.

1950

North Korea invades South Korea on June 25, igniting the Korean War. The US Air Force plays an integral role in the conflict.

1965

The US Air Force begins Operation Rolling Thunder during the Vietnam War.

1976

Women are admitted to the US Air Force Academy for the first time.

1990

Operation Desert Shield in Iraq begins on August 7.

2001

In October the US Air Force delivers the first retaliatory blows for the September 11 terrorist attacks in Operation Enduring Freedom in Afghanistan.

ESSENTIAL FACTS

DATE OF FOUNDING
September 18, 1947

MOTTO
Aim High . . . Fly-Fight-Win

PERSONNEL (2013)
330,000 active duty members
100,000 Air National Guard
190,000 civilian employees

ROLE
The role of the US Air Force is to fly, fight, and win in air, space, and cyberspace. Members of the air force pilot and maintain aircraft, including fighters, bombers, and planes that serve in many other roles. The US Air Force is also responsible for security in cyberspace, critical military satellites, and the nation's nuclear deterrent force.

SIGNIFICANT MISSIONS

Atomic bombing of Hiroshima and Nagasaki, 1945

Operation Rolling Thunder, 1965

Operation Desert Shield, 1990

Operation Enduring Freedom, 2001

WELL-KNOWN AIRMEN

William "Billy" Mitchell served in World War I and advocated for strong airpower.

Henry "Hap" Arnold prepared the air forces of the United States for World War II.

QUOTE

"Integrity first, Service before self, Excellence in all we do."—*from the core values of the US Air Force*

GLOSSARY

AVIONICS
Electronics designed for use in an aircraft.

BIPLANE
An aircraft with two wings, one usually set above the other.

CALIBRATE
To set up a measuring device so its measurements will be accurate.

CIVILIAN
A person who is not a member of the military.

COALITION
A group working together, such as a group of nations fighting a war together.

COCKPIT
The area of a plane where the pilot sits.

COURT-MARTIALED
Brought to a military trial to face charges of breaking military laws.

DOGFIGHT
A midair battle between two planes.

FLEET
A group of military ships that move and work together.

INSUBORDINATION
Resistance to authority.

INSURGENT
An armed rebel.

INTELLIGENCE
A collection of information that has military or political value.

LASER
A device that produces a narrow, powerful beam of light and which is often used in weapon targeting systems.

MONOPLANE
An aircraft with one wing.

MUNITIONS
Ammunition.

PARATROOPER
A soldier who parachutes from an airplane.

RECONNAISSANCE
Scouting or surveying, especially in wartime.

SORTIE
A mission.

SURVEILLANCE
Close watch over.

ADDITIONAL RESOURCES

SELECTED BIBLIOGRAPHY

Budiansky, Stephen. *Air Power: The Men, Machines, and Ideas That Revolutionized War, from Kitty Hawk to Gulf War II*. New York: Viking, 2004. Print.

Tapper, Jake. *The Outpost: An Untold Story of American Valor*. New York: Little, 2012. Print.

FURTHER READINGS

Earl, Sari. *Benjamin O. Davis Jr.: Air Force General & Tuskegee Airmen Leader*. Minneapolis, MN: Abdo, 2010. Print.

Winchester, Jim. *Modern Military Aircraft*. San Diego, CA: Thunder Bay, 2004. Print.

WEBSITES

To learn more about Essential Library of the US Military, visit **booklinks.abdopublishing.com**. These links are routinely monitored and updated to provide the most current information available.

PLACES TO VISIT

MUSEUM OF AVIATION

Robins Air Force Base
Warner Robins, GA 31088
478-926-6870
http://www.museumofaviation.org

The museum takes visitors through the history of aviation as told through military aircraft.

NATIONAL MUSEUM OF THE UNITED STATES AIR FORCE

1100 Spaatz Street
Wright-Patterson Air Force Base
Dayton, OH 45433
937-255-3286
http://www.nationalmuseum.af.mil

The museum, which includes a large-screen theater, features aircraft and historical displays dealing with the entire history of the US Air Force.

SOURCE NOTES

CHAPTER 1. AERIAL RESCUE UNDER FIRE

1. Richard Lowry. "Incoming: Firefight at COP Keating." *Examiner.* Examiner, 16 Nov. 2009. Web. 1 Apr. 2014.

2. "September 11 Anniversary Fast Facts." *CNN.* CNN, 11 Sept. 2013. Web. 1 Apr. 2014.

3. Tom Bowman. "Battle in Afghanistan Highlights Bravery, Failures." *NPR.* NPR, 16 Apr. 2010. Web. 1 Apr. 2014.

4. Mike Cronin. "North Fayette Captain Saves US Troops in Afghanistan Battle." *TribLive.* Trib Total Media, 23 Nov. 2009. Web. 1 Apr. 2014.

5. Jill Laster. "Pilot Honored for Organizing Airstrikes." *Air Force Times.* Air Force Times, 19 Feb. 2014. Web. 1 Apr. 2014.

6. Captain David Faggard. "Airman over Firefight: 'I Won't Forget Them As Long As I Live.'" *US Air Forces Central Command.* US Air Force, 15 Oct. 2009. Web. 1 Apr. 2014.

7. Joe Paisley. "Former AFA Goalie Polidor Honored with Distinguished Flying Cross." *Gazette.* Gazette, 28 May 2010. Web. 1 Apr. 2014.

8. Jill Laster. "Pilot Honored for Organizing Airstrikes." *Air Force Times.* Air Force Times, 19 Feb. 2014. Web. 1 Apr. 2014.

CHAPTER 2. AIRBORNE

1. Mary Hoehling. *Thaddeus Lowe: America's One-Man Air Corps.* Chicago, IL: Kingston, 1957. Print. 107–109.

2. "Pancho Villa." *Encyclopaedia Britannica.* Encyclopaedia Britannica, 2014. Web. 1 Apr. 2014.

3. Scott S. Smith. "Gen. Billy Mitchell Gave the Air Force Its Wings." *Investor's Business Daily.* Investor's Business Daily, 11 Mar. 2013. Web. 1 Apr. 2014.

4. John T. Correll. "The Legend of Frank Luke." *Air Force Magazine.* Air Force Magazine, Aug. 2009. Web. 1 Apr. 2014.

5. "Manfred, Baron von Richthofen." *Encyclopaedia Britannica.* Encyclopaedia Britannica, 2014. Web. 1 Apr. 2014.

CHAPTER 3. EARNING THEIR WINGS

1. "Fact Sheet: Pearl Harbor." *Naval History & Heritage Command.* US Navy, n.d. Web. 1 Apr. 2014.
2. "James H. Doolitle." *Encyclopaedia Britannica.* Encyclopaedia Britannica, 2014. Web. 1 Apr. 2014.
3. "Berlin Airlift." *History Channel.* History Channel, 2011. Web. 1 Apr. 2014.

CHAPTER 4. HIGH-TECH AIRPOWER

1. "Iraqi Death Toll." *Frontline.* PBS, 2014. Web. 1 Apr. 2014.
2. "Air Force Performance in Operation Desert Storm." *Frontline.* PBS, 2014. Web. 1 Apr. 2014.
3. "Our Team." *US Air Force Thunderbirds.* US Air Force, 2014. Web. 1 Apr. 2014.
4. Ibid.
5. "AIM-120 AMRAAM Slammer." *Military Analysis Network.* Federation of American Scientists, 14 Apr. 2000. Web. 1 Apr. 2014.
6. "Air Force One." *The White House.* The White House, n.d. Web. 1 Apr. 2014.
7. "US Air Force – Fiscal Year 2014 Budget Overview." *US Air Force.* US Air Force, April 2013. Web. 1 Apr. 2014.
8. "Summary of the DOD Fiscal Year 2014 Budget Proposal." *Department of Defense.* Department of Defense, n.d. Web. 1 Apr. 2014.

CHAPTER 5. THE AIR FORCE TODAY

1. "United States Air Force Posture Statement." *Department of the Air Force.* US Air Force, 28 Feb. 2012. Web. 1 Apr. 2014.
2. "Museum Location." *National Museum of the US Air Force.* US Air Force, n.d. Web. 1 Apr. 2014.

CHAPTER 6. TEAMWORK

1. "Air Force Combat Controllers." *US Military.* About.com, 2014. Web. 1 Apr. 2014.
2. Maria Goodavage. "Letting Slip the Real Dogs of War." *Wall Street Journal.* Wall Street Journal, 25 Feb. 2012. Web. 1 Apr. 2014.

CHAPTER 7. CAREERS IN THE AIR FORCE

1. "Air Force Personnel Demographics." *US Air Force Personnel Center.* US Air Force, n.d. Web. 1 Apr. 2014.
2. Eve Dumovich. "True Trailblazers." *Boeing Frontiers.* Boeing, 8 Mar. 2008. Web. 1 Apr. 2014.
3. "The Air Force in Facts and Figures." *US Air Force.* US Air Force, May 2013. Web. 1 Apr. 2014.
4. "Air Force Personnel Demographics." *US Air Force Personnel Center.* US Air Force, n.d. Web. 1 Apr. 2014.
5. "Global Horizons." *Armed Forces Journal.* Armed Forces Journal, 1 Aug. 2013. Web. 1 Apr. 2014.
6. "Commissioned Officer Training." *US Air Force.* US Air Force, 2013. Web. 1 Apr. 2014.

CHAPTER 8. LIFE IN THE AIR FORCE

1. "Air Force ROTC." *North Carolina A&T State University.* North Carolina A&T State University, Sept. 2013. Web. 1 Apr. 2014.

2. "US Air Force Academy." *US News & World Report.* US News & World Report, 2014. Web. 1 Apr. 2014.

3. "FAQs." *US Air Force Academy.* US Air Force Academy, n.d. Web. 1 Apr. 2014.

4. "US Air Force Academy Outcomes." *US Air Force Academy.* US Air Force Academy, 2009. Web. 1 Apr. 2014.

5. "Enlisted Pay." *US Air Force.* US Air Force, n.d. Web. 1 Apr. 2014.

6. "Officer Pay." *US Air Force.* US Air Force, n.d. Web. 1 Apr. 2014.

7. "Retirement." *US Air Force.* US Air Force, n.d. Web. 1 Apr. 2014.

INDEX

ABOUT THE AUTHOR

Robert Grayson is an award-winning former daily newspaper reporter and the author of books for young adults. Throughout his journalism career, Grayson has written stories on historic events, the military, sports figures, arts and entertainment, business, and pets. These stories have appeared in national and regional publications, including *New York Yankees* magazine and *NBA Hoop*. He has written books about the Industrial Revolution, the American Revolution, the California gold rush, animals in the military, and animal performers, as well as the environment, law enforcement, and professional sports.